St Albans

IN OLD PHOTOGRAPHS

An aerial view of St Albans, showing the relationship between the Roman city in the valley and the later medieval town on top of the hill around the great Norman abbey, *c*. 1938. St Alban is believed to have been tried in the Roman theatre and then led up the hill, along what is now Fishpool Street, to his execution. This was already a venerated place by the end of the Roman period, and when urban life began again in the late Saxon period or after the Conquest it was around the abbey, leaving the site of the Roman city for archaeologists to rediscover many centuries later.

St Albans

IN OLD PHOTOGRAPHS

SAM MULLINS

Alan Sutton Publishing Limited
Phoenix Mill · Far Thrupp · Stroud
Gloucestershire

First Published 1994

British Library Cataloguing in Publication Data.
A catalogue record for this book is available from
the British Library.

ISBN 0-7509-0120-9

Typeset in 9/10 Sabon.
Typesetting and origination by
Alan Sutton Publishing Limited.
Printed in Great Britain by
Hartnolls, Bodmin, Cornwall.

Front cover: Market day in front of the Town Hall, 1895. A stall selling plants and ferns is attracting interest from two ladies and a child.

Contents

Introduction

This is the first book of historic photographs of St Albans for several years, bringing into the light many images previously unpublished or recently collected by St Albans Museums. A major reason for this selection is to encourage more photographs to be brought into the public domain. Photographs provide the most vivid evidence of the passing of time and of the changing face of our surroundings. In streets which are familiar to modern eyes we can see transport based on the horse, citizens in frock coats, crinolines or hob-nailed boots and lost buildings and views, as well as evidence of continuity such as market stalls, the restoration of churches, civic ceremony and archaeological investigation.

St Albans Museums have in recent years begun to actively seek out photographic evidence of both the recent and the more distant past. In compiling this book it was immediately obvious that huge areas of the city remain undocumented in public collections. This book's concentration on the abbey, the historic city centre and Verulamium reflects the bias and strengths of the image collection, but also shows its deficiencies in recording the commonplace rather than the extraordinary. The selection also demonstrates the primary use to which photography was then put, the making of postcards and souvenirs. The eastern side of St Peter's Street, being less picturesque, seems to have consistently escaped the camera, as in general have the inner suburbs around Mount Pleasant, in Fleetville, surrounding Clarence Park, and even important streets such as London Road and Victoria Street. We would like to make the collections more geographically comprehensive and consequently get to know more of the city's nooks and crannies during the age of the camera.

Other than the postcard view, the camera has always tended to be used to record the extraordinary or the unusual rather than the commonplace. Hence in this selection we see the shopfront and the proprietor but never the inside arrangements, the shoppers making their purchases or the rooms where stock was stored or goods prepared. St Albans' great abbey was extensively recorded before and during its Victorian restoration but we have no record of a Sunday morning congregation at its portals, let alone the nave packed with worshippers. The image included here of Lee's shoe manufactory is one of the very few documentary records of St Albans at work.

Nevertheless a rich record of St Albans in the period up to 1939 is available for which we have to thank the city's professional photographers such as Cherry, postcard manufacturers such as Valentines but above all collectors such as Kent and the first honorary curators of the then Hertfordshire County Museum (now the Museum of St Albans) who wisely bought or even commissioned high quality photographs of the city which, even then, they realized was changing fast. Nearly a century later that pace of change has quickened. Up until the Second World War it was still possible to view St Albans as a country market town a motor bus ride away from London. The move of both people and businesses out of London since the war has expanded the city's size and radically changed its function. This selection records the city up to that point. The change in the townscape has to be looked for quite hard in many of the views, suggesting that this attractive, historic city has survived the passage of time reasonably intact, and there do seem to be few significant losses documented here.

If you have interesting or early photographs of St Albans, bring them in to show us at the Museum of St Albans in Hatfield Road (tel. 0727 819340). If you do not wish to part with them, they can be copied and enlargements made before being returned. We would also be interested to hear from anyone who would like to become involved in the care and documentation of the collection on a voluntary basis.

Sam Mullins
St Albans, 1994

From the air, the long, narrow triangular shape of St Peter's Street running from St Peter's Church to the abbey can be easily recognized, c. 1938. Probably dating from the early Middle Ages, the street was deliberately laid out as a market place, before the shops between Market Place and Chequer Street encroached on this large open space.

Market Place on a busy day, *c.* 1914.

Market Day

This view shows the eastern side of Market Place on market day, looking towards St Peter's Street with the mass of the Town Hall just visible on the far right.

Looking down Market Place towards the High Street on market day, *c.* 1900. Note the large gas globes to light the shops on the right.

The market in full flow, Market Place, *c.* 1880. Brightman's sold locally produced vegetables from this pitch for many years.

Baskets of celery and rhubarb are among other vegetables for sale in Market Place, *c.* 1910.

Market Place, *c.* 1925. This view shows a fruit and vegetable stallholder setting up for market opposite the impressive butcher's premises of Steabben & Son, with a butcher's high cart outside collecting deliveries.

The market stalls have yet to spread out in front of the Town Hall, *c.* 1905.

A bustling Market Place, *c.* 1905.

Livestock market, St Peter's Street, *c*. 1915.

Saturday market. In the 1920s the market has yet to spread up St Peter's Street, but has now occupied the area in front of the Town Hall.

A good show of livestock in St Peter's Street, 1925, much of it destined for the Christmas dinners of St Albans. Livestock markets had been held in the broad end of St Peter's Street in front of the Town Hall for centuries. The cattle market moved to Drover's Way, now the site of multi-storey car-parks, in 1926.

Market day, St Peter's Street, 1938. The street market has been an important feature of the city's life since Saxon times. Note how the market has gradually spread up St Peter's Street from Market Place during the twentieth century.

The market, *c.* 1900. These stalls, including Pratt's florists stall, are outside the front of the Town Hall. Note how rough the street surface is. The street market has long been a lively and important part of the city's attraction.

Resurfacing work on St Peter's Street, *c*. 1905.

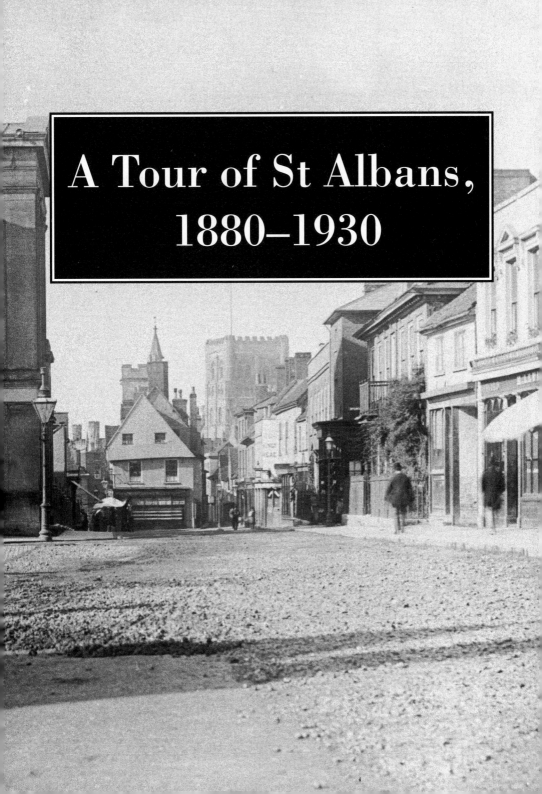

A Tour of St Albans,
1880–1930

On a quiet occasion, a few pedestrians and a cart load of hay is all there is to be seen in Market Place, *c.* 1910. Note the loose road surface before the introduction of tarmacadam.

French Row, looking down the narrow street from what is now the entrance to Christopher Place, *c.* 1905.

French Row. Local tradition has it that this narrow and picturesque street derives its name from the mid-fourteenth century when, following his defeat at the battle of Poitiers, King John II of France was imprisoned here, but there is no evidence to support this. It was pedestrianized in 1976.

French Row. The timber-framed buildings originated around 1400 as the 'Christopher' inn. By *c.* 1910, when this photo was taken, they were occupied by the Clock Tower Toilet Club, the function of which remains a mystery.

A delivery van of the City of London Flour and Grain Company waits on 'Mayle's Corner', the corner of Verulam Road and George Street, in the 1880s.

A busy day in Market Place, *c*. 1910. Note the two butcher's carts outside Steabben's the butchers.

Market Place, 1920.

A.J. Dorrell's premises on the left once formed a fitting centre point for the High Street. Note also the fountain on the right, designed by Scott in 1874 and restored today in the Victoria Square office complex by the city station.

High Street, *c.* 1910. The town's main street looks the part with well-appointed shops, an absence of traffic and granite set crossings to keep pedestrians' feet clean while crossing the street.

The Fighting Cocks public house, *c.* 1886. This unusual building claims to be the oldest inhabited pub in the country. Its hexagonal structure is derived from a pigeon house moved in around 1600 from the grounds of the dissolved abbey up the hill.

Before Telford's construction of Verulam Road in 1825, George Street was the main road into the town from the north-west, and before the rise of St Peter's Street, between the wars, was one of the city's principal shopping streets. It remains an attractive street of largely medieval buildings behind later fronts.

George Street looking up the hill towards the High Street, 1905. The street is named after the medieval George inn.

Inn yard of the George, George Street. The George traced its origins as an inn to at least 1401, although it ceased to be a hotel around the time of the First World War, shortly after this photo was made for sale particulars. The frieze over the arch, now lost, is said to have come from Holywell House.

In the centre, 13 Fishpool Street with decorated plaster or pargeting, and on the right the entry to the Crow public house, 1899.

The middle portion of Fishpool Street, with the Lower Red Lion just beyond the street lamp, 1893. This street's fine heritage of Georgian carved doorcases is well in evidence.

The long curve of Fishpool Street makes it one of the most attractive streets in the country. The street's characteristic blue brick raised pavements can be contrasted with the muddy metalled road surface in around 1900.

Fishpool Street. It is difficult to imagine today's well-preserved and exclusive street as one of the town's poorest areas at the turn of the century. Fishpool Street's poverty was also its saviour as many of its cottages and elegant houses survived unaltered into the conservation era.

Looking up Fishpool Street from the junction with Branch Road, *c.* 1910. The cottages on the right next to the Blue Anchor were demolished in 1935.

St Michael's Bridge and Kingsbury Mill, *c.* 1910. The ford over the River Ver was used at this point during the Roman period for the road to Colchester (Camulodunum). This postcard shows Kingsbury Mill in operation.

St Michael's Bridge, *c.* 1910. Children paddle in the River Ver. In the background is Kingsbury Mill and to the right Kingsbury Manor House. The bridge is the oldest surviving in use in Hertfordshire and was built in 1765.

Verulam Road and Christ Church, *c.* 1880. In the background is Christ Church, today converted into offices (see also p. 99). Note the loose surface of one of the city's major through roads at this time.

Christ Church, Verulam Road, *c.* 1900.

The ground floor of the Clocktower was designed to be leased as a shop when it was built in *c.* 1405. In 1915 it was occupied by G. Pearce, a saddle and harness-maker.

Market day, *c.* 1904. Market Place is busy with a great variety of horse-drawn traffic. Note the Red Lion inn on the left and the Fleur de Lys next to it with its carriage entrance.

Peahen crossroads, *c.* 1910. A peaceful scene looking down Holywell Hill, one of the city's busiest points today. In the 1950s, at the crossing of the A5 and A6 trunk roads, this was reckoned to be one of the busiest crossroads in the world, and the first traffic lights in the county were installed in response to frequent accidents at this spot.

Peahen crossroads looking towards Chequer Street during the First World War. Look for the soldiers in uniform and the military policeman keeping an eye on them to the left of the policeman on point duty.

Peahen crossroads looking towards the High Street. Note the soldiers with a large dog on the street corner.

Holywell Hill, *c.* 1920. The top half of the street has always been an important retail location.

Holywell Hill looking up the hill from Sopwell Lane, *c.* 1925.

This aspect of Holywell Hill, past the Duke of Marlborough public house, has changed little since around 1900.

Sopwell Lane, originally the main road to London, c. 1910.

London Road looking towards Peahen crossroads, with the Peahen Hotel on the corner and its extensive stabling to the left, *c.* 1910. Note the horse-drawn omnibus picking up passengers in the High Street.

Peahen crossroads, always a busy junction, at the convergence of the main roads later known as the A5 and A6, *c.* 1920.

London Road, *c.* 1910. This postcard shows the city's eastern suburbs, a view remarkably similar to today's.

From the city station bridge, 1915. The tree-lined aspect of Victoria Street is very different to today's street.

Green's department store occupied a series of shops on the west side of Chequer Street, *c.* 1905.

St Peter's Church and Green, *c.* 1905.

St Peter's Street on a winter's day, *c.* 1900. 'Merely Mary Ann' was the attraction at the County Theatre through the arch next to the County Club on the left. Marks & Spencer's store occupies the site today.

St Peter's Street was St Albans' principal street in the early 1930s, the halcyon days of the private bus operator.

Hall Place, St Peter's Street from the north, 1904. Fixed to the wall, there is an advertisement for the sale of this medieval house and its outbuildings (to the left) for redevelopment.

St Peter's Street, mid-1880s. The city's principal street, shortly after the planting of the trees which remain such a distinctive and pleasant feature of the city centre.

Market day in front of the Town Hall, *c.* 1914.

The elegant Victorian pavilion in Clarence Park, designed by Mr Ford, the city surveyor.

Clarence Park, 1894

The city was gifted Clarence Park by Sir John Blundell Maple MP, proprietor of Maple's, the fashionable London furniture store. The park was opened in 1894 by the Duke of Cambridge in a celebration dampened but not spoiled by heavy rain.

A view across the park from the zig-zag path by the railway bridge towards the back of the pavilion, with the bandstand in the middle distance, 1894. On the far side of the park, the lodge, by the main gates, looks out on to Clarence Park Road which awaits the building of its elegant Edwardian houses.

Clarence Park Lodge and main entrance, taken shortly after the park opened. This was the park superintendent's house with a small refreshment room attached for the sale of 'non-intoxicating liquors'.

The bandstand was a regular venue for Sunday afternoon concerts. It was a rustic construction with a roof thatched in heather.

The fountain was the gift of Lady Blundell Maple.

The pavilion has been completed and work is proceeding on the cinder cycle and running tracks which surrounded the cricket square. This view probably dates from shortly before the opening of the park.

A festive group of St Albans school teachers poses for the camera at the 1897 Jubilee celebrations in Clarence Park.

St Albans City Football Club team of 1912/13 in front of the pavilion at Clarence Park with the fruits of one of their most successful seasons: the Bingham-Cox Cup, the Spartan League Championship and the Herts Charity Cup.

Staff of Adey and White's Brewery behind Chequer Street, *c.* 1900.

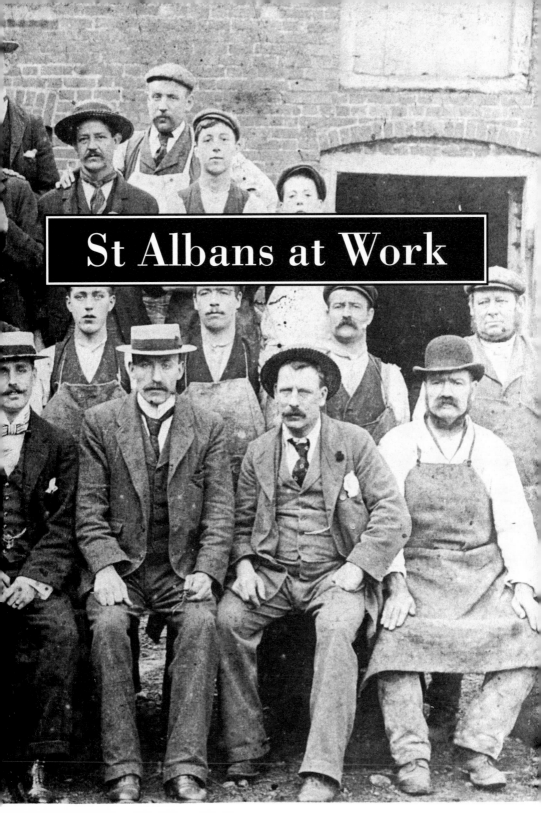

St Albans at Work

Workroom at a hat factory, location unknown. The manufacture of hats, associated generally with nearby Luton, was also an important industry in St Albans up to the First World War.

Workroom at a St Albans hat factory; again the location is unknown.

Edwin Lee's boot and shoe factory, Grosvenor Road, 1927.

The meadows of St Albans and Hertfordshire were important sources of hay for the millions of horses stabled in London. Two loads of hay and straw from Butterwick Farm, Smallford, are seen here in the Haymarket, London.

F.C. Simpson, boot repairer, outside his house and workshop at 37 Culver Road, St Albans, *c.* 1930.

A view across St Michael's village, with the Kingsbury Mill at work grinding corn on the right, *c.* 1915.

A postcard showing the Fighting Cocks pub and the Silk Mills, *c.* 1910. In the Middle Ages this was the site of the Abbey Mills, used to grind grain. In the eighteenth century the water power was harnessed to spin silk and, with the addition of a steam engine, the site was a manufactory until 1938. Some of the mill buildings survive and have recently been converted for residential use.

Maddox's shop, St Peter's Street, decorated for Queen Victoria's Diamond Jubil...ee,

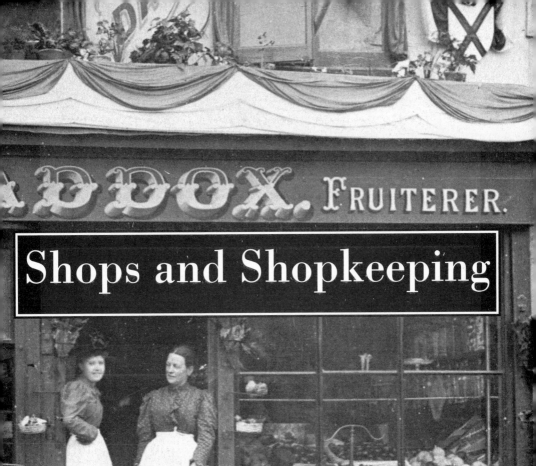

DDOX. FRUITERER.

Shops and Shopkeeping

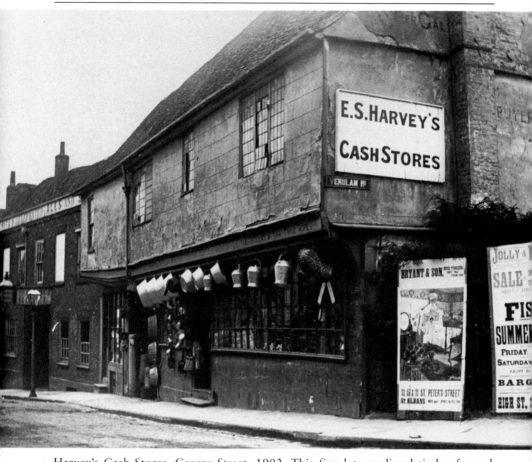

Harvey's Cash Stores, George Street, 1902. This fine late-medieval timber-framed building is today the Tudor Tavern. The building dates from around 1500 and is one of the city's finest late-medieval buildings.

Hallam's shop after a fire. Although the cause of the fire is not known, Hallam's stock of lamp oils would have been highly inflammable. The shop, on the corner of Chequer Street and High Street, was rebuilt and Hallam's branched out to include general hardware, gas fitting and plumbing. It is occupied today by General Accident.

Hedges' wonderful shopfront display shows the varied stock of the shoe shop, including hobnailed boots, at 17 High Street, opposite the Clocktower, *c.* 1907.

Pearce's fishmonger's and fruiterer's shop, *c.* 1910. This photograph has the shop's staff posed in front of the fish slab. The shop was next to the Clocktower.

Gibbs & Bamforth's premises at the corner of Market Place and Upper Dagnall Street, *c.* 1900. They were booksellers, stationers and proprietors of the *St Albans and Herts Advertiser*. The building dates back to the mid-sixteenth century and was built as the town hall for the newly formed borough of St Albans. It remained the meeting place of the mayor and corporation until the Town Hall was built in 1830.

The old town hall from Upper Dagnall Street, *c.* 1885. The printing works of Gibbs & Bamforth occupied the building behind.

On the left is the Corn Exchange, built in 1857; in the centre is the attractive timber-framed building known as The Gables, occupied here in around 1885 by Roberts the chemist; to the right is the façade and entry of the Duke of Wellington public house.

The Gables, Market Place. The shop was occupied by the chain footwear store, Freeman, Hardy & Willis, one of the city's earliest multiple stores, c. 1890.

Market Place, 1897. Worsell the drapers were about to vacate The Gables; Boots then threatened the shop with demolition until public pressure saved the historic building. Next door was Symington & Son, 'clothiers, tailors and juvenile outfitters; sole agents for Vine & Co's Butchers Clothing'.

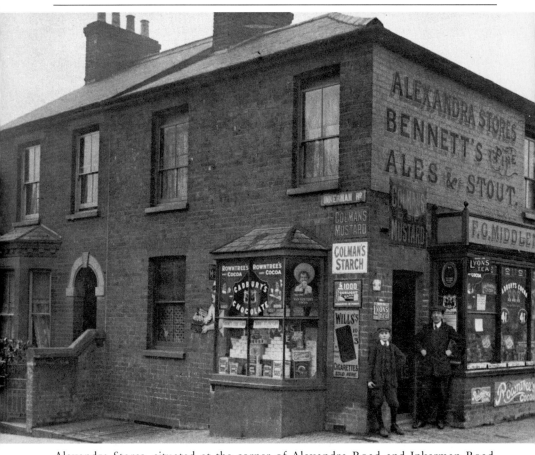

Alexandra Stores, situated at the corner of Alexandra Road and Inkerman Road, *c.* 1910.

Fisk & Son was the city's other major drapery store, beginning life further down the street and later adding No. 17 and several other premises along the High Street. No. 17 was saved from demolition by Fisk's after public protest in 1911.

An early Christmas publicity photograph for the St Peter's Street branch of Sainsbury's. Note the turkeys are sold with their necks on.

Pearce's fishmonger's and fruiterer's shop, Market Place, *c.* 1930. A fine spread of fresh fish and fruit are on show next to the Clocktower. This had once been the site of the Rose and Crown public house.

Osborne Bros, George Street, today occupied by Stuart Warton, goldsmith.

Fox's chemist's shop on the corner of Hatfield Road and Clarence Park Road, *c.* 1920.

St Peter's Street, 1913. This view shows a London General Omnibus Co. 'B' type bus on the 84 route from London to St Albans, established the previous year.

St Albans Abbey from Kingsbury, *c.* 1900.

St Albans Abbey:
Restoration and Rebuilding

Waxhouse Gate, also known as School Lane from when St Albans School occupied the Lady Chapel of the abbey, *c.* 1880. A candlemaker's premises was once situated in the gate or close by, lending its name to the lane.

St Albans Abbey, east end, *c.* 1880. The garden has flourished: the fruit trees on the east end of the Lady Chapel are in leaf, several rows of peas are in evidence and some salad vegetables have already been cropped.

Here, in 1868, the east end still awaits restoration and the diversion of the footpath and the enlargement of Sumpter Yard has yet to disturb the immaculately tended garden, early in its season, which runs right up to the east window.

St Albans Abbey before the restoration of 1880, showing the west front of the abbey massively propped by the architect Gilbert Scott against its collapse. The original perpendicular west front was built in the time of Abbot John of

Wheathampstead (1420–40) and controversially rebuilt by Sir Edmund Beckett, 1st Baron Grimthorpe in 1880–3, who proclaimed the old work 'thoroughly good for nothing'.

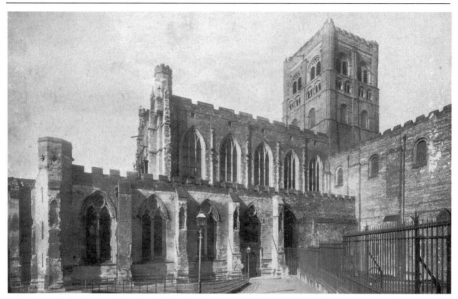

St Albans Abbey, north side of Lady Chapel. The public passageway through the east end of the abbey was boarded up in 1874 to facilitate the restoration work inside. This action caused great controversy as it stopped up an important public right-of-way and resulted in the passageway being forcibly opened on the night of 20 May 1874. Eventually a compromise was reached in 1878 when land at the east end of the abbey was purchased and the footpath diverted around it.

An unusual view of the abbey from the Holywell Brewery, situated off Holywell Hill behind the Peahen Hotel. It was one of four Victorian breweries in the town, the others being Adey & White's in Chequer Street where the Maltings are today, the Kingsbury Brewery at the far end of Verulam Road and the St Peter's Brewery in St Peter's Street, behind where Mothercare is today.

The public passageway through the abbey from north to south came out just opposite the cedar tree on the south side of the Lady Chapel. Proposals to block this useful right-of-way were violently opposed in 1874.

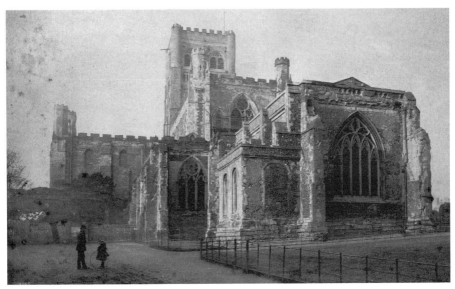

The path round the east end was created in 1878 shortly before this photo was taken. The restoration of the Lady Chapel was begun in 1880.

Built between 1420 and 1440, the perpendicular west front was one of the glories of the medieval abbey. It was swept away and replaced in the restoration by Grimthorpe of 1880. This early photo of *c.* 1870 shows its unrestored state and, in front, the unreformed churchyard.

The west end of the abbey was completely redesigned and rebuilt as part of Grimthorpe's restoration. This view of 1885 shows a heap of rubble awaiting removal.

St Albans Abbey from the north-east before 1888. This view looks across Waxhouse Gate and what is now Heritage Close towards the abbey church, where scaffolding can be seen as work proceeds on the north aisle. This card was bought as a souvenir from Allen's Fancy Bazaar, 20/21 St Peter's Street.

The restored abbey from the north, probably taken from the top of the Clocktower. This photograph shows the terrace of cottages in School Lane beyond Waxhouse Gate which was demolished for the building of Heritage Close.

St Albans Abbey nave looking east. During the restoration work in the 1880s, a temporary timber screen was erected from the top of the rood screen to the ceiling to keep out dust and the noise of the work from the rest of the church. Services were conducted within the nave, rather than from the high altar.

St Albans Abbey choir and rood screen after the restoration. The nave was reopened following the restoration in 1885. The pulpit on the left was designed by Grimthorpe but the first bishop refused to preach from it, calling it a 'rotunda'. It was eventually dismantled in 1972 and stored. The pews are also Grimthorpe's work.

St Albans Abbey rood screen and organ. The rood screen divided the medieval abbey church, separating the monks' church to the east from the laity's church or nave to the west. The stone screen was built between 1350 and 1400. The splitting of the organ in 1908 enhanced the view of the chancel arch from the nave.

A patriotic postcard of the abbey interior during the First World War.

Destroyed at the Reformation and rediscovered in fragments and restored in 1872, the Purbeck marble shrine of St Alban was the culmination of a series of shrines for the saint. Pieces of the shrine were discovered during restoration work and it was carefully reassembled in its original position behind the high altar. A further restoration in 1993 included more fragments found since 1872 and, together with its elaborate embroidered cover, the shrine to Britain's first Christian martyr still attracts the devotion of pilgrims and the wonder of visitors.

St Stephen's Church, *c.* 1860.

The Churches of St Albans

St Michael's Church before restoration, *c.* 1888. The tower and west end of the church are about to be swept away by Lord Grimthorpe's restoration of 1898, which saw this tower demolished and replaced by a new one to his own design offset to the north.

St Michael's Church before restoration, *c.* 1890. This interesting church is one of the three parish churches said to have been founded by Abbot Ulsinus in AD 948. Certainly the nave and chancel walls date back to the tenth century and include both Saxon masonry and re-used Roman brick. Jessamine Cottage in St Michael's Street is visible on the far side of the churchyard. Note also the unusual grave boards in the churchyard.

St Michael's Church before restoration. The old village schoolroom is to the left.

The interior of St Michael's Church looking eastwards following the restoration of the church, *c.* 1910.

A man mows the churchyard grass, *c*. 1880. The original tower of St Michael's Church is in the background.

After the dissolution of the monasteries in 1539, Sopwell Nunnery was bought by Sir Richard Lee and converted into a private mansion. Sopwell Lane can just be seen to the right at its junction with Old London Road in this photograph of 1898.

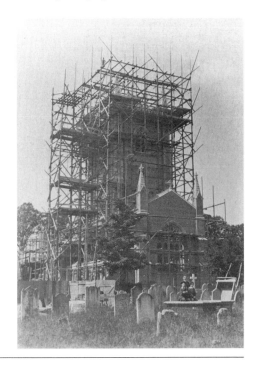

Lord Grimthorpe's restoration in 1894–5 made St Peter's a wholly Victorian building, adding a new west front, north aisle, tower and chancel. In this view the scaffolding is still in place and the churchyard as yet uncleared.

An interesting view across St Peter's Green to the church before Grimthorpe's restoration work of 1894–5. Note one of the public water pumps in the centre of the green.

St Peter's Church before restoration, 1890. The poor state of the church can be readily seen. Both transepts had been pulled down in 1802 and the exterior rendered to prevent further decay of the stonework.

An interior view of St Peter's Church before restoration, showing the western gallery and organ, 1893.

St Peter's Church. An interior view after restoration, 1908.

St Paul's Church, on the corner of Blandford Road and Hatfield Road, while under construction, 1909.

The Tabernacle Baptist Church, Victoria Street, 1880.

Christ Church, Verulam Road, *c.* 1880. Built in 1850 as a Roman Catholic church, it was supposedly a copy of Parker's Archangel Raphael church at Surbiton. This ambitious building in the Italian Renaissance style was endowed by Mrs Worley, who gave her name to the nearby street. It had been taken over by the Church of England by the time of this photograph.

These well-dressed ladies may have been sewing comforts for troops during the First World War.

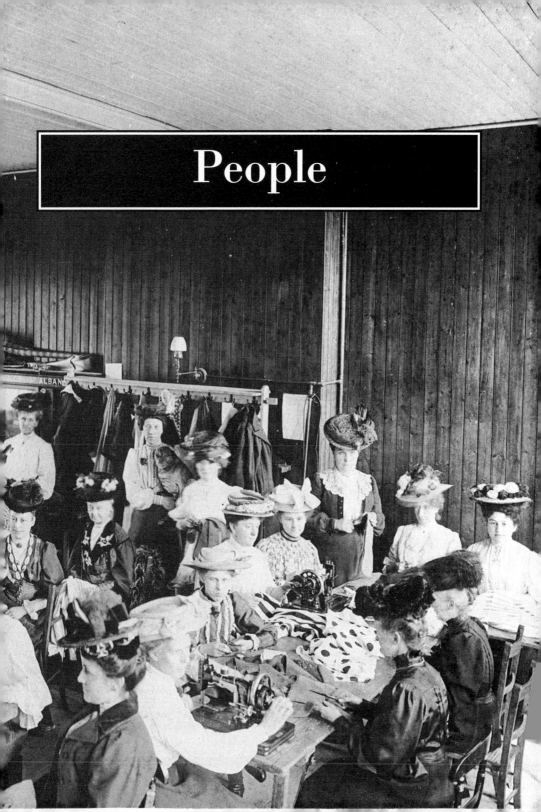

People

Garden Fields School, Group 6, *c.* 1900.

Bernard Street School, Class No. III, *c.* 1900.

Bernards Heath Infants School, 1906/7. The headmistress, Miss Mitchell, is on the right at the front, holding the bell which she rang at her desk to gain silence in class. Everyone is in their Sunday best, with the girls resplendent in lace pinafores and some of the boys in sailor suits or lace collars.

School group at Alma Road School, 1923.

An outing from the Blue Anchor in Fishpool Street, 1920s. The picture is a large advertisement for Benskins Brewery to whom the pub belonged.

A police band, *c.* 1908. The postcard message reads, 'my dearest mother, A & I went to the concert, this is a p.c. of the band that played and the hero . . . is the one sitting on the left hand side of the fat man with the drums'.

Opening of the City Library, 1910. The Scottish benefactor, Mr Andrew Carnegie, is seen presenting a model of the new library in Victoria Street to the mayor, Cllr Dr Eustace H. Lipscombe, at a ceremony in the council chamber in the Town Hall.

A posed harvest picture taken after the corn harvest had been cut and stooked.

Farming

The area where Verulamium Park is today was rich grazing and meadow land until sold to the city corporation by the Earl of Verulam in 1929. This view of unknown date shows a herd of bullocks grazing the River Ver meadows.

A set-piece harvest picture, perhaps taken after the harvest is in as all appear to be in their best clothes. The men did the cutting and the women raked up and turned the hay. Note the horse-drawn mower on the left and the harvest cart on the right.

Hay meadows below Belmont Hill, c. 1905. This view from the River Ver below the Holywell Hill bridge across the meadows, with lower Holywell Hill on the left, shows Belmont Hill on the right where just one pair of houses has been built. The hay crop is being mown by hand with scythes.

A field of ripening corn, c. 1900. This photograph was taken on St Germain's Farm, part of Verulamium Park from 1929 and site of Roman Verulamium many centuries before.

Turning the mown hay above the old St Michael's vicarage and parish church, *c.* 1900. Today this field is within Verulamium Park.

Getting in the hay harvest on what is today the running track at Westminster Lodge but was then the rich meadowland of St Germain's Farm, *c.* 1905. The boys have been taken away from school to help with the harvest.

The St Albans Pageant, 1907.

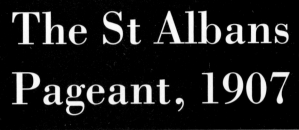

The St Albans
Pageant, 1907

A studio portrait of William Webster Hoare, a Druid in episode I of the pageant, taken by M. & A. Austin, St Albans.

Mrs C.H. Ashdown as Lady Anne Bacon in the final episode.

Violet Burton in the role of one of Boudicca's wild women.

Enid and Eric Langham Simpson, Saxon peasants in episode IV.

An ancient British chariot demonstration outside the Red Lion Hotel in the High Street.

Medieval knights show their paces in the High Street, watched by a huge crowd.

The Sea God Mosaic of around AD 180, Verulamium, 1930s.

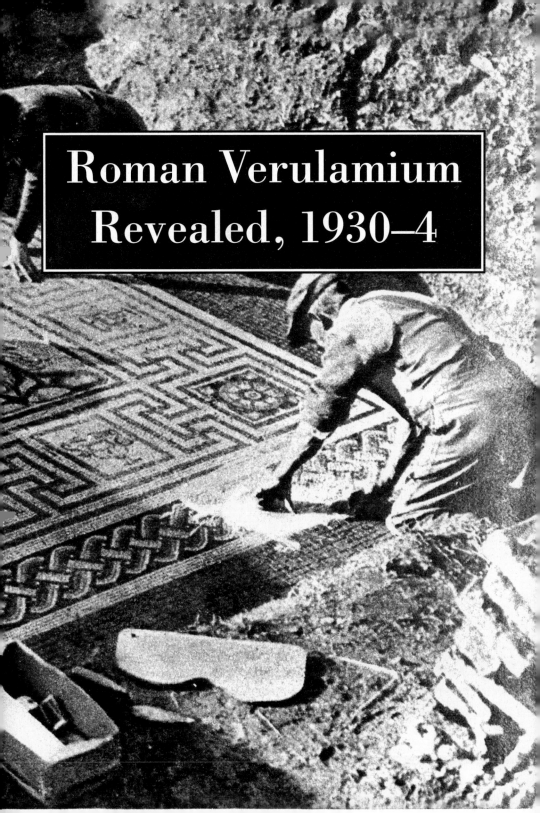

Roman Verulamium Revealed, 1930–4

Wheeler's campaigns unearthed a number of fine and well-preserved mosaic floors. The shell mosaic is one of the most striking, and today forms the central feature of the Verulamium Museum. It was excavated from beneath a hedgeline in 1930.

The painted wallplaster in the room of this Roman house survived to over a metre high when discovered in 1931.

Mortimer Wheeler and assistants washing pottery. The work at Verulamium attracted huge public interest as witnessed by the crowd behind the fence, and progress reports were a regular feature in the national newspapers of the day.

Mortimer Wheeler with workmen investigating a well. The purchase of Verulamium Park in 1929 by the city council allowed a major excavation campaign by Wheeler in 1930–4, one of the first systematic examinations of a Roman city in this country.

A posed photograph for the press, with no labourers other than befrocked girls in evidence.

The digging team. The heavy work was done by these manual labourers and the finer trowelling by students.

The museum was established to show the finds excavated at Verulamium during the 1930s. The opening ceremony is being performed by the Earl of Harewood on 8 May 1939. The official party, being welcomed by the mayor outside the museum doors, are (from left) the town clerk, the mayor (standing at microphone), Princess Mary (the Princess Royal, younger sister of George VI), the Earl of Harewood and the mayoress.

Three of the finest Roman mosaics from Verulamium were lifted and relaid in the new museum, seen here shortly after its opening in 1939. The mosaics are in the same position today although the displays were expanded and modernized in 1991.

St Peter's Street from the top of the Town Hall, *c.* 1895.

Lost St Albans

The Little Red Lion, High Street, *c.* 1880. A carriage turns out of Market Place into the High Street past one of Adey & White's many tied public houses in the city. These three buildings were originally medieval lock-up shops. The two on the right were demolished to expand Fisk's premises in 1911.

An almost unbelievably rural Sandpit Lane, before the city began to expand out into the countryside, *c.* 1920.

Looking down St Michael's Street, *c.* 1900. Visible on the extreme right is the Victorian farmhouse of St Germain's Farm, demolished before the building of the Verulamium Museum in 1938–9.

Hall Place, 1904. This large house with medieval features stood in St Peter's Street immediately north of St Peter's Church. Henry VI is said to have been brought here after the Lancastrian defeat at the first Battle of St Albans in 1455.

An other view of Hall Place, which was demolished in 1907 to make way for the Edwardian housing development of Hall Place Gardens.

The causeway, Verulamium. The construction of the lake in Verulamium Park has completely altered this view, which looks past Ver Cottage across what is now the end of the lake and down the causeway to the chimney of the Silk Mill.

The demolition of Thorpe & Collings' premises in the High Street was a great loss. The building, which dated from around 1700, provided a centre-piece for the street. Unusually, the upper storeys were built out over the pavement and supported on cast-iron columns.

Acknowledgements

The compiler is indebted to all those who have donated, or loaned for copying, photographs and postcards to the Museum of St Albans over the years and to the colleagues in St Albans museums who have assisted with information for the captions. Any inadvertent inaccuracies or omissions are entirely the compiler's responsibility.